Copyright © 2017 by Nisha Todd
All rights reserved. No Part of this
book may be reproduced or transmitted
in any form or by any means, electronic
or mechanical, including photocopying,
recording, or by any information storage
and retrieval system, without written permission
of the publisher

www.nishajayne.co.uk

INTRODUCING... #SNAPHAPPY

This journal is all yours. Be creative and jot down all of those ideas floating around your head. Let's make some awesome photos together!
It is time to plan your very own FASHION SHOOT.

This is a book for you to learn something new and create something great!

A special place for those pretty, cool and crazy photos you are about to take.

This Journal Belongs to:

#SELFIE

NAME:..................................

FIRST THINGS FIRST

WHAT IS YOUR IDEA? YOU NEED TO DO SOME RESEARCH! COLLECT PICTURES THAT YOU LIKE FROM MAGAZINES, BOOKS OR ONLINE AND STICK THEM HERE! WRITE SOME IDEAS DOWN AND THEN LET THEM GROW.

COULD YOU PLAN A SHOOT BASED ON A FAVOURITE SONG? OR MAYBE YOU WANT TO TURN SOMEONE INTO A MERMAID?! ANYTHING IS POSSIBLE IN A FASHION SHOOT AS LONG AS YOU WANT TO CREATE IT.

MIND MAPS & MOODBOARDS ARE A GREAT WAY TO THINK CREATIVELY AND FOCUS YOUR IDEAS. LET'S START WITH A MIND MAP...

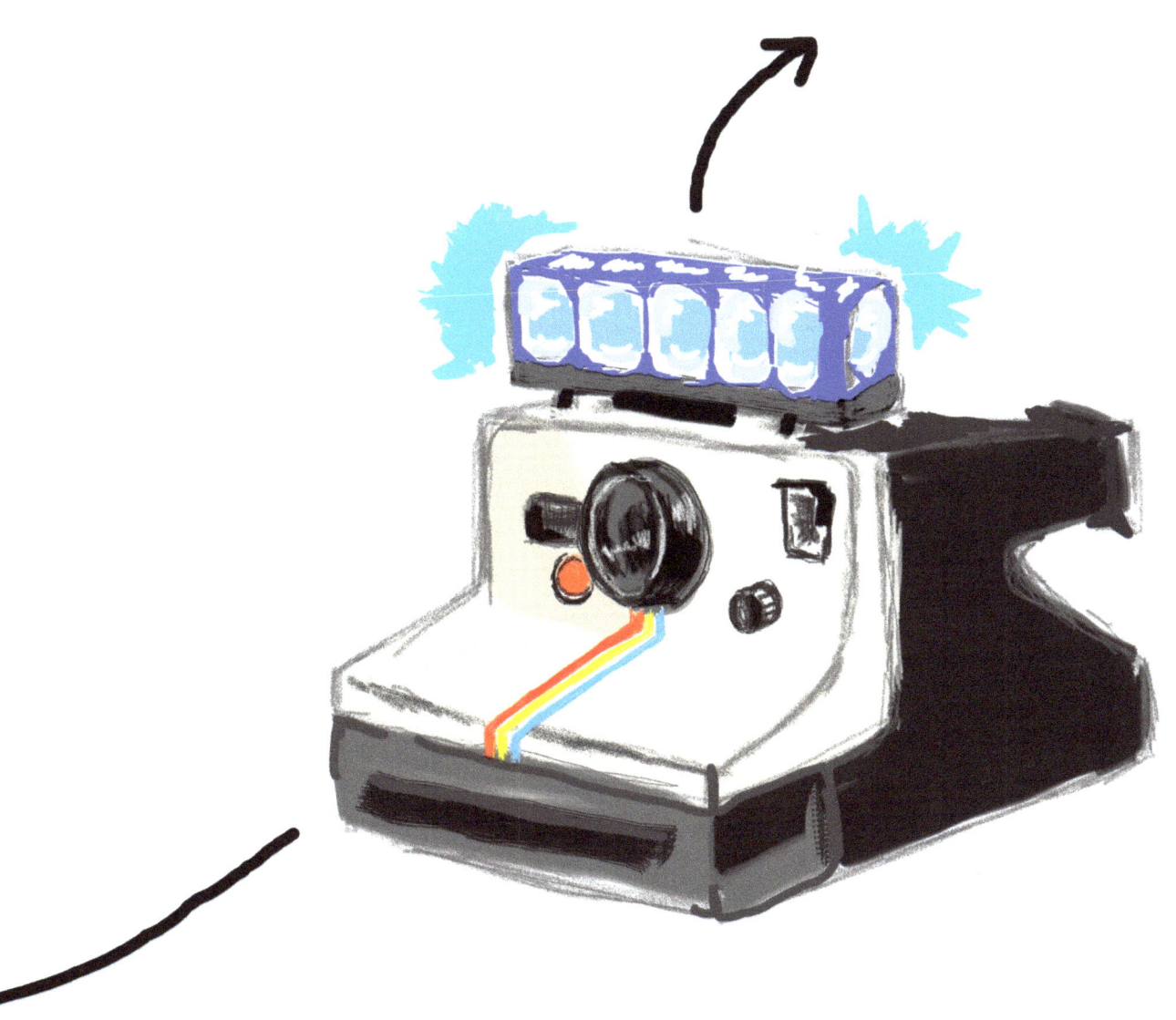

MOODBOARD

GO FOR IT! STICK ALL THOSE IDEAS DOWN. TEXTURES, COLOURS, OUTFITS, MAKE UP IDEAS POSES, CUTOUTS! WHATEVER INSPIRES YOU! THIS IS WHERE IT GOES!

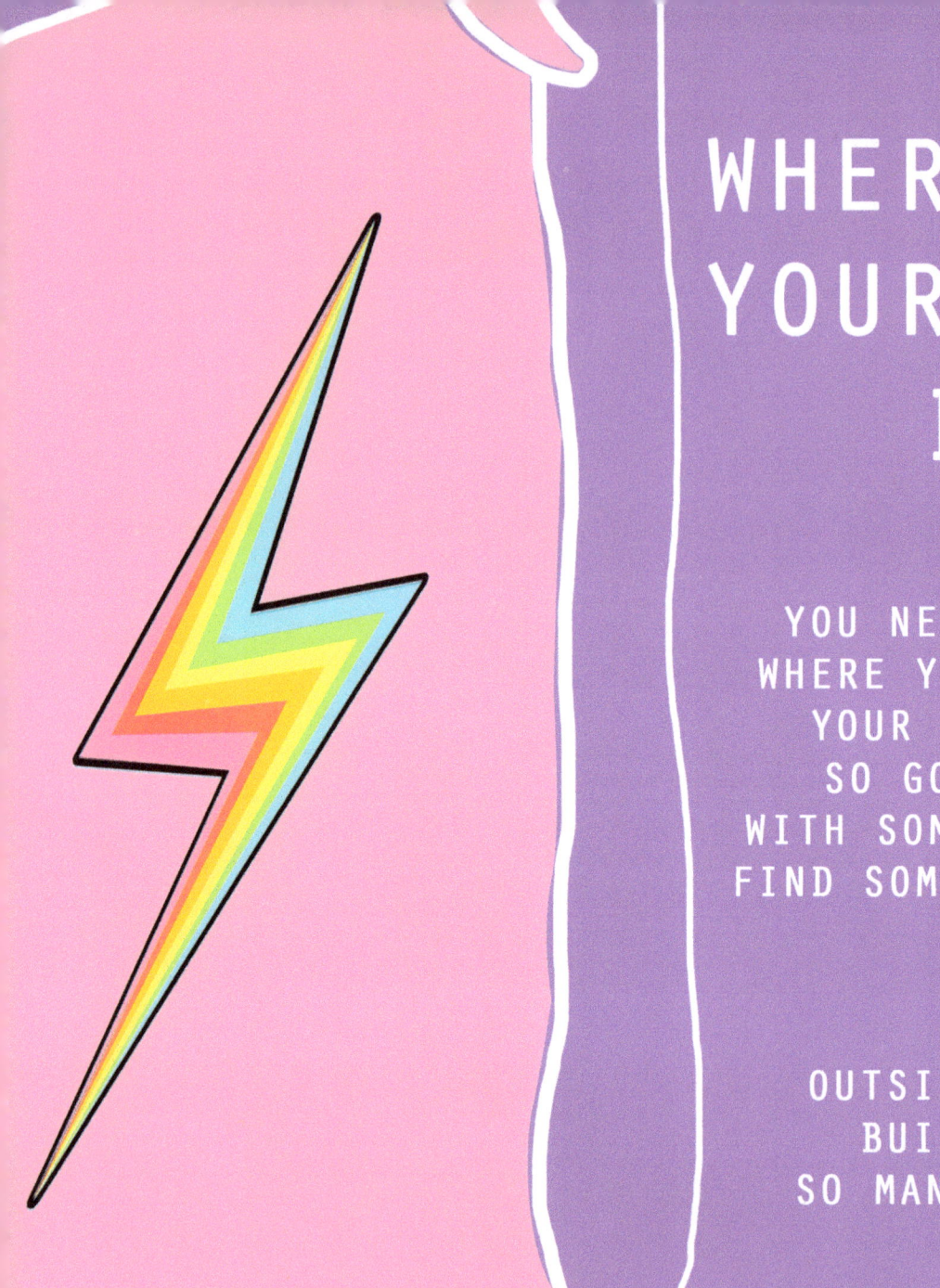

WHERE WILL YOUR SHOOT BE!

YOU NEED TO DECIDE WHERE YOU WANT TO DO YOUR PHOTOSHOOT! SO GO EXPLORING WITH SOME FRIENDS AND FIND SOME COOL PLACES.

OUTSIDE? INSIDE? BUILD A SET? SO MANY CHOICES!!

TAKE SOME SNAPS OF ALL THE PLACES YOU
FIND AND STICK THEM IN HERE.
ONCE YOU HAVE COMPARED THEM ALL
DECIDE ON YOUR FAVOURITE
AND CARRY ON PLANNING!

FILL THESE PAGES WITH AWESOME PLACES!

YOU MIGHT EVEN FIND AN AWESOME COLOURED WALL!

THE CREATIVE TEAM

OK SO YOU HAVE DONE YOUR MINDMAP AND YOUR MOODBOARD! YES! NOW IT'S TIME TO GET YOUR GIRL GANG INVOLVED...OR GO SOLO... IT'S UPTO YOU. BUT IT IS HARD TO DO EVERYTHING, SO I ADVISE GETTING YOUR FRIENDS INVOLVED. IT IS TIME TO BUILD YOUR CREATIVE TEAM.

ON A FASHION SHOOT EVERYONE HAS THEIR OWN ROLES! SO LETS START MATCHING UP YOUR FRIENDS TO ALL OF THE DIFFERENT JOBS NEEDED TO CREATE AN AWESOME FASHION SHOOT!

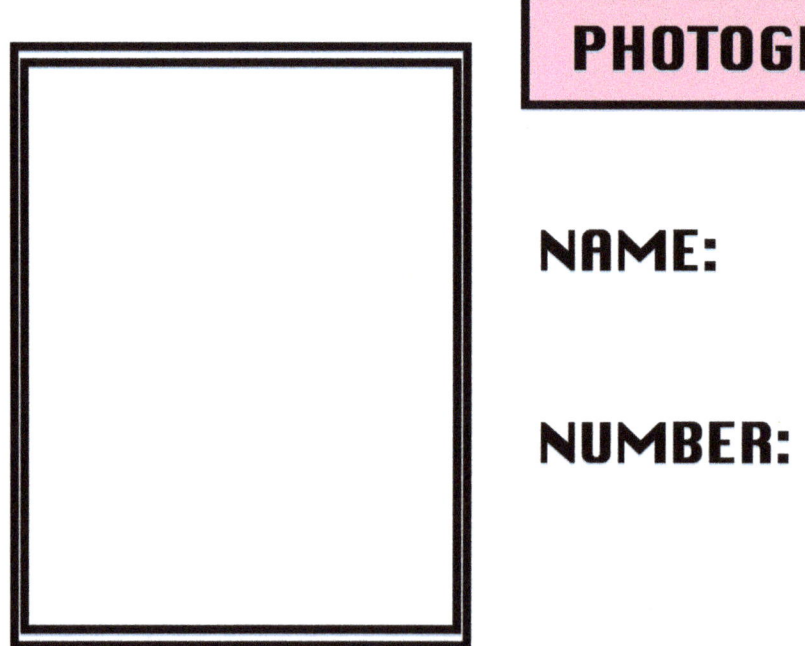

PHOTOGRAPHER

NAME:

NUMBER:

STYLIST

NAME:

NUMBER:

HAIR & MAKE UP

NAME:

NUMBER:

SET DESIGNER

NAME:

NUMBER:

MODEL

NAME:

NUMBER:

you got this Girl!

Time to create the CALL SHEET!

A Call Sheet is created for every shoot. It is sent to everyone involved in the shoot so that they know who is who and so that they can contact everyone.

It also has the schedule for the photoshoot!

Here is where you list the time you start (call time) and then when you will be shooting, your breaks and when you plan to finish.

It is a summary of the day!

Heres one for you to fill in for your photoshoot.

SNAPHAPPY
CALL SHEET

Shoot Name:
Location:
Date:

CONTACTS

Photographer:
Stylist:
Hair & Make up artist:
Set designer:
Model:

Schedule

Call Time:

Shooting Time:

Lunch:

Shooting time:

Finish! :

...THERE IS SOMETHING CALLED A SHOT LIST...

When you are shooting your awesome idea you don't want to be shooting the same thing over and over again!

You need to make it interesting.

One easy way to make sure you cover all the awesome details is to make a shot list.

In fashion there are some general guidlines of what shots you will need to make your shoot work in a magazine layout.

I am going to write a list for you and when you are shooting make sure you have it handy so that you can tick off the shots as you go!

BE SURE TO ADD ANY MORE IMPORTANT SHOTS TO THE LIST!
A FASHION SHOOT USUALLY HAS 8 OUTIFT CHANGES!
SO BE SURE TO CHANGE OUTFITS FOR THE SHOTS.

SHOT LIST

- [ ] **A COVER SHOT**

(A PORTRAIT THAT WOULD LOOK GOOD ON A MAGAZINE COVER!)

- [ ] **DOUBLE PAGE SPREAD**

(SOMETHING THAT WOULD LOOK GREAT ACROSS TWO PAGES)

- [ ] **DETAIL SHOT**

(A CLOSE UP OR A STILL LIFE OF ACCESSORIES)

- [ ] **FULL LENGTH SHOT**

(SHOW YOUR AWESOME MODEL OFF FROM HEAD TO TOE!)

- [ ] **SET THE SCENE**

(A LANDSCAPE? WIDE SHOT THAT SHOWS OFF THE GREAT SCENE)

- [ ]
- [ ]
- [ ]

TIME TO STORYBOARD

It's time to draw!!!

Let's start your storyboard,
where your ideas turn into drawings,
which will turn into photos!

It's a good idea to storyboard a shoot
because it is a visual shot list.

It helps you decide on compositions!

You can set up your photo to be like your sketch
and then experiment after that.

But it always gives you a fab starting point.

So go go go... draw the photos you are planning
to take!

COVER SHOT

THE FULL LENGTH SHOT

DOUBLE PAGE SPREAD IDEAS

DETAIL SHOTS

ANOTHER AWESOME SNAP

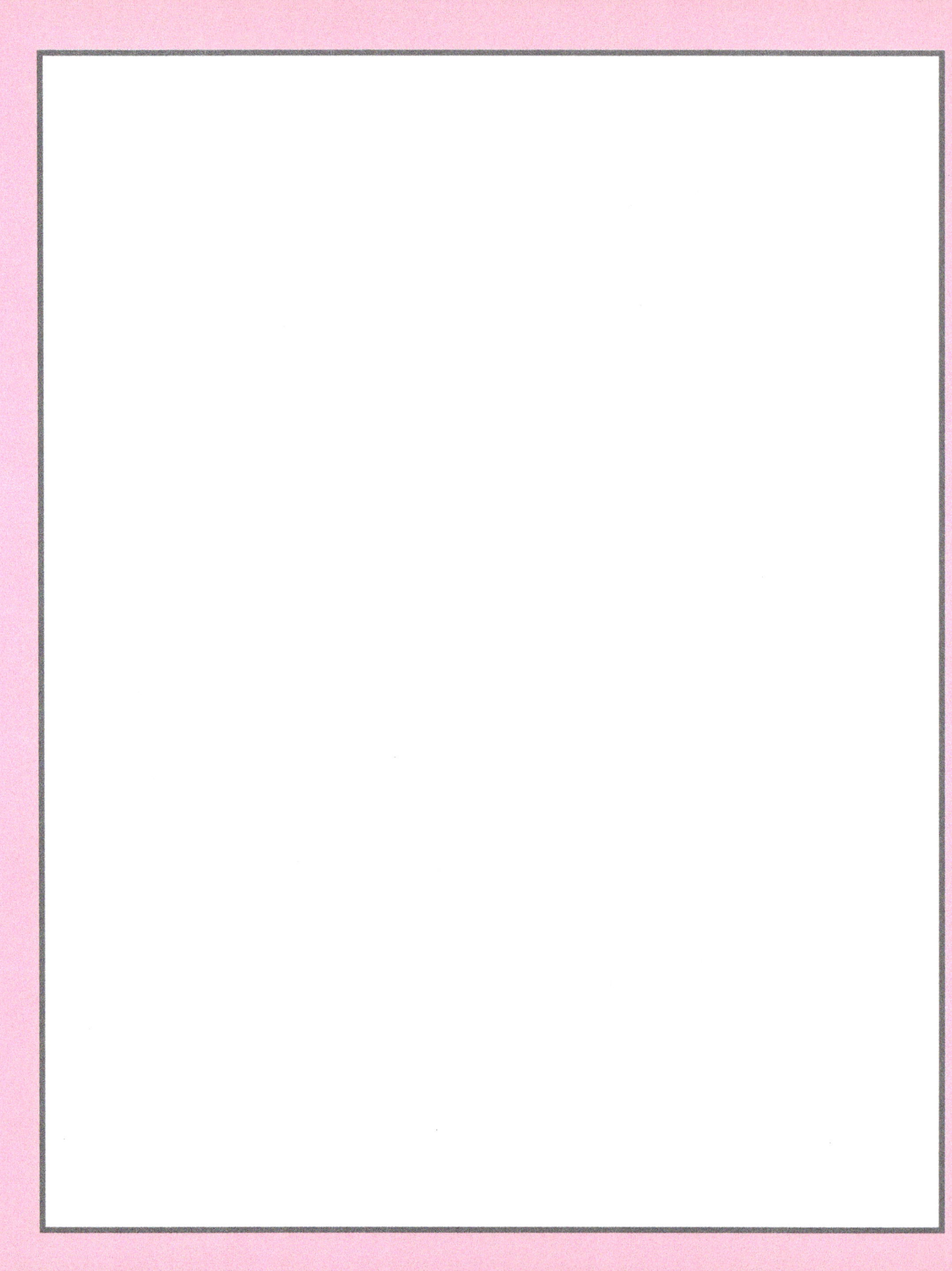

NOW SEE WHAT ALL YOUR DRAWINGS LOOK LIKE TOGETHER!

DRAW THEM HERE IN ORDER SO YOU CAN SEE HOW YOUR WHOLE SHOOT WILL LOOK

EQUIPMENT LIST

....BIG CHOICES....
WHAT ARE YOU GOING TO SHOOT WITH?
WELL ANYTHING THAT CAN TAKE A PHOTOGRAPH!
WE CAN'T ALL HAVE THE CAMERA WE WANT RIGHT AWAY.
SO IF YOU HAVE A CAMERA THEN USE IT!
IF YOU DON'T THEN HOW ABOUT A PHONE?
OR IF YOU WANT TO HAVE SOME REAL EXCITEMENT
YOU COULD USE A FILM CAMERA!!!

If you go for the digital camera option then great you can point and shoot and click away!

If you want to use your phone well it works just the same way! Be sure to shoot in a place with a lot of natural light...(outside is always a good option)

If you have a chance to shoot on film then that is really exciting. You won't even know what your photos will look like until they are developed! So you must take your time to choose exactly what you want to shoot and to make sure everything is on the right settings. Depending on the film you will only have a limited amount of photographs that you can take!

If you decide to shoot on film i recommend a
Lomography camera!
These are great little plastic cameras that
come in awesome designs.

(Put one on your christmas list!!!!)

Also if you're worried about using film don't be!
I am sure there is someone you can ask who has used it before and
if not just follow the instructions or google it!

DIY PHOTOGRAPHY TIPS

HERE ARE SOME LITTLE DIY TIPS THAT YOU CAN USE IN YOUR PHOTOSHOOT!

Cut out some great shapes from cardboard to use as props! You can paint them or use coloured cards. Literally make anything you want to!

All of these props are made from paper!

So firstly a reflector is something most photographers use! It reflects light!

You can make one at home, all you need to do is get a large piece of cardboard and wrap it in foil, then tape the foil to it on the back.

You now have your very own reflector! Just move it around until you see the sun reflect onto your models face!

Use any great piece of material you can find. Do you have a cool curtain or bedsheet? You can clip this up somewhere and use it as a backdrop.

lights

Lights!!! You can use anything! Lamps are great for mood lighting! You can use coloured bulbs to create colourful lights and fairy lights are always fun!!

today is the day!

date: _____

So go ahead...
Go for it and take lots of pictures!
Lets see what you create!

Have Fun
Take your time
Enjoy your awesome
photoshoot

how did it go?

Once you have finished taking all of your photos go and get them printed!

We have some special pages coming up for them!

Next is EDITING...
Print all of the photos that you took on a few pieces of paper. These are called contact sheets!

Once you have stuck them in here you can circle all of your favourite shots and then print these a bit bigger to decide on your final collection of photos that tick off your shot list.

Here's an example of one of my contact sheets.

If you shot on film you will need to get your film scanned or ask the shop to make you a contact sheet.

Or get them all printed small and sort them into piles of what you like or dont like.

stick your contact sheet here

stick your contact sheet here

stick your contact sheet here

The chosen Ones

Hopefully you have decided on your final
photographs and there is nothing
missing from the shot list.

Print all of the circled photos and lay them out
in order. Bet they are looking great!!!!

Move them around until they match your storyboard
or if you find a better order for them then use that.

Now it is time to stick them here in order!

Make those pages look Amazing!!!!

Use stickers, draw around them,
Cut them into cool shapes,
Be creative and have fun!

Cover Photo Here

STICK YOUR PHOTOS IN AND HAVE FUN!

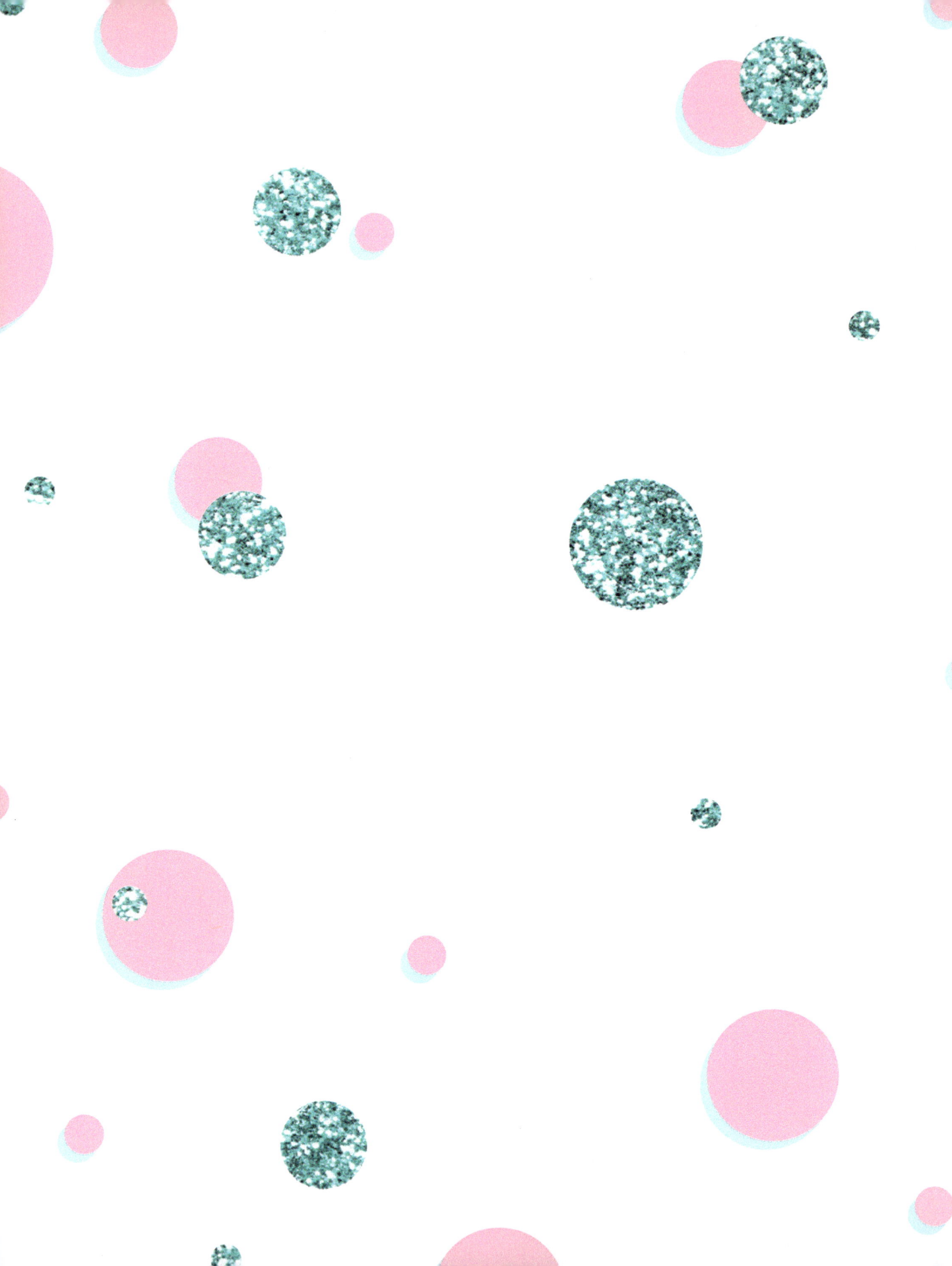

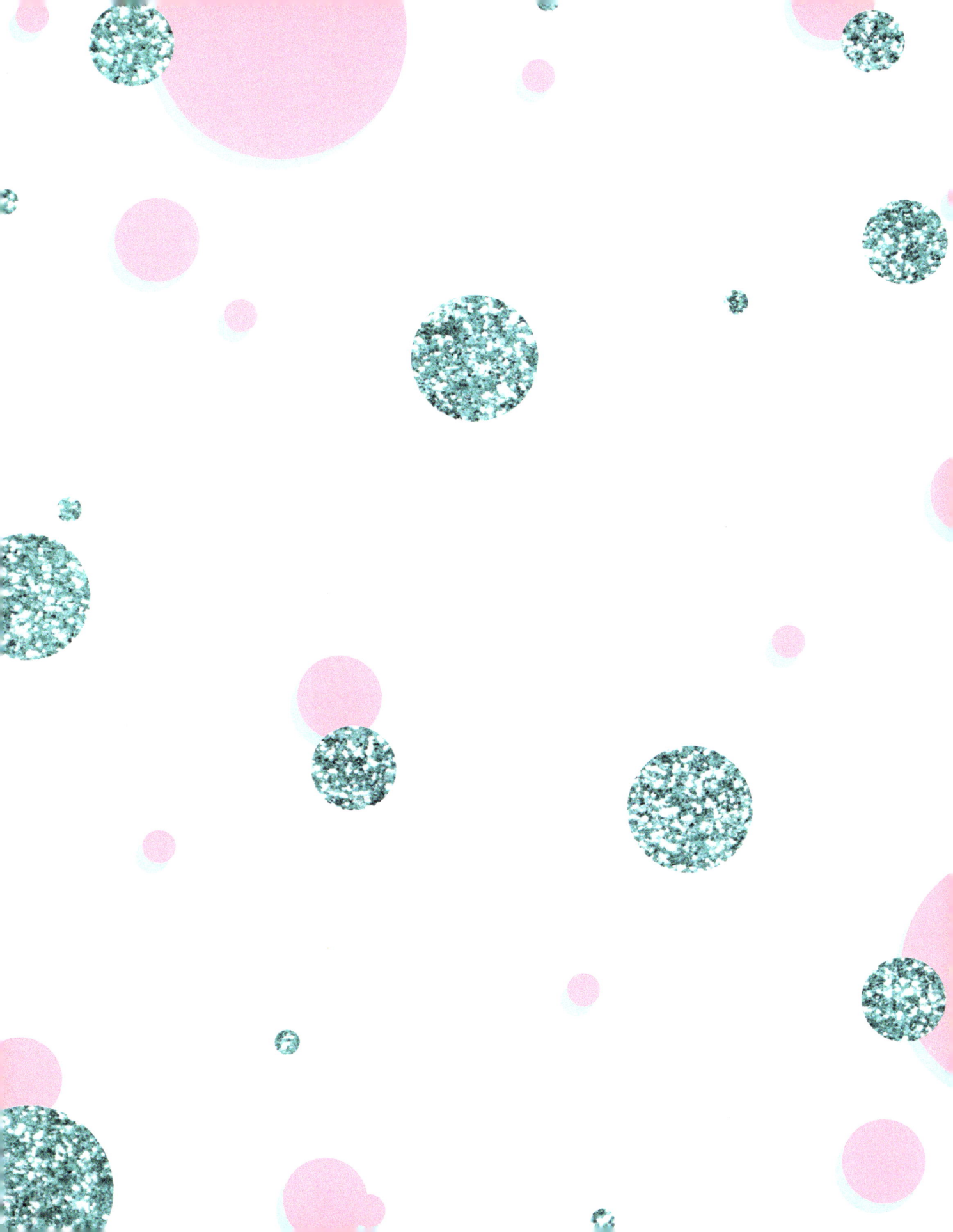

YAY
Your first Photo shoot
is complete.
!AMAZING!
Keep taking photos
have fun and stay
!AWESOME!

www.ingramcontent.com/pod-product-compliance
Lightning Source LLC
Chambersburg PA
CBHW061151070526
44584CB00034B/4481